W9-BIE-028

NATIONAL FOOTBALL LEAGUE

★★★★★ **NFL** ★★★★★

GREATEST

# SUPER BOWL & NFL RECORDS

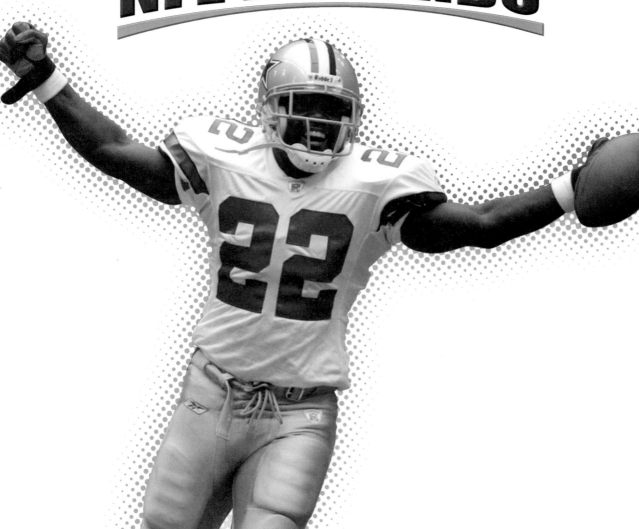

## By James Buckley, Jr.

### SCHOLASTIC INC.

New York    Toronto    London    Auckland    Sydney
Mexico City    New Delhi    Hong Kong    Buenos Aires

All photos © **Getty Images**.

**Front cover (clockwise)**: Pool, Andy Lyons, George Rose

**Back Cover**: Harry How

**Interior**: Title page Stephen Dunn; (4) Nick Laham; (5) Simon Bruty, Stephen Dunn, George Rose, Jonathan Daniel, Jim McIsaac; (6) Nick Laham; (7) Jim Rogash, Tony Duffy, Jeff Gross; (8) Streeter Lecka; (9) Ronald Martinez, Jonathan Daniel, M. David Leeds; (10, 11) Jeff Gross; (12) George Rose; (13) Jeff Gross, Nick Laham, Stephen Dunn; (14) Harry How; (15) Jed Jacobsohn; (16) Stephen Dunn; (17) George Rose, Doug Pensinger, Stephen Dunn; (18) Rick Stewart; (19) Elsa, Rick Stewart, Mike Powell; (20) Jim McIsaac; (21) Rick Stewart, Lisa Blumenfeld; Otto Gruele Jr; (22) Dilip Vishwanat; (23) Donald Miralle, Lisa Blumenfeld, Rick Stewart; (24) Geroge Rose; (25) Streeter Lecka, George Rose; (26) Jonathan Daniels; (27) Ronald Martinez; Kevin C. Cox; Otto Greule Jr; (28) Elsa; (29) Rick Stewart, Ronald Martinez; (30) Elsa; (31) Jim McIsaac, Stephen Dunn, Doug Pensinger; (32) Tim Pidgeon, Doug Pensinger

ISBN-13: 978-0-545-06544-3
ISBN-10: 0-545-06544-5

Published by Scholastic Inc.
SCHOLASTIC and associated logos are trademarks and/or registered trademarks of Scholastic Inc.

12 11 10 9 8 7 6 5 4 3          8/0

Designed by Cheung Tai
Printed in the U.S.A.
First Scholastic printing, August 2008

# Contents

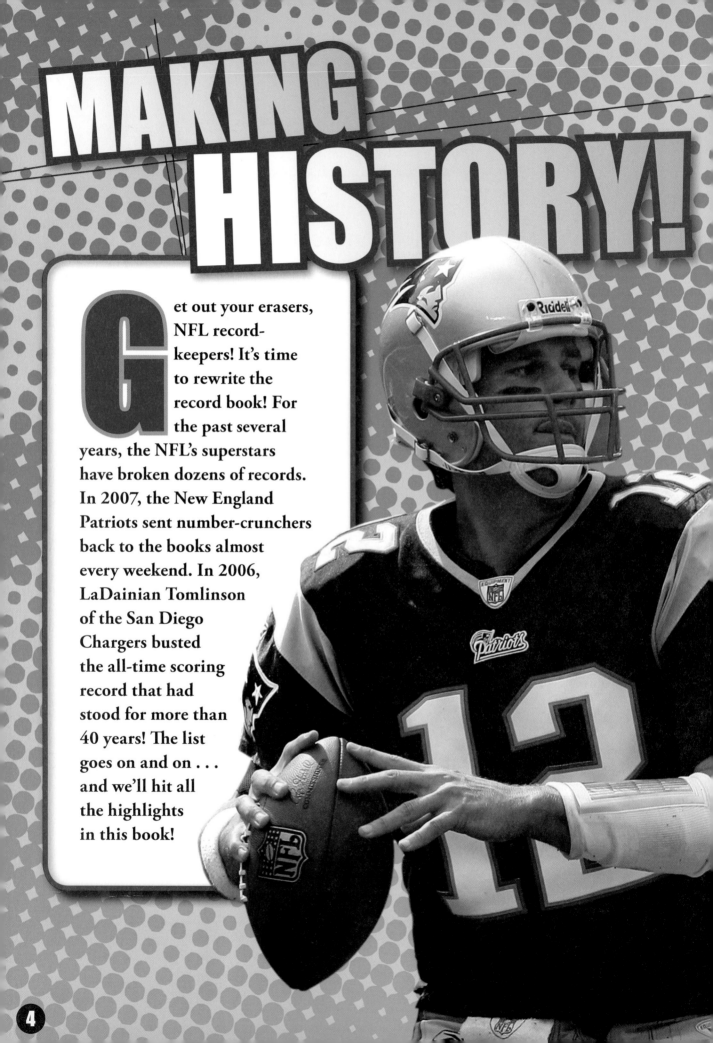

# MAKING HISTORY!

**G**et out your erasers, NFL record-keepers! It's time to rewrite the record book! For the past several years, the NFL's superstars have broken dozens of records. In 2007, the New England Patriots sent number-crunchers back to the books almost every weekend. In 2006, LaDainian Tomlinson of the San Diego Chargers busted the all-time scoring record that had stood for more than 40 years! The list goes on and on . . . and we'll hit all the highlights in this book!

## VOICES FROM THE PAST

The NFL has featured the world's best football players for more than 80 years. Today's players look to players from the past to show just how great they are. Tom Brady of the New England Patriots wouldn't be a record-setter unless Johnny Unitas and Dan Marino had come before him. Devin Hester's amazing return records would be nothing special without Gale Sayers as role model. Inside, we'll meet today's great record-setters as well as some of the heroes that came before them.

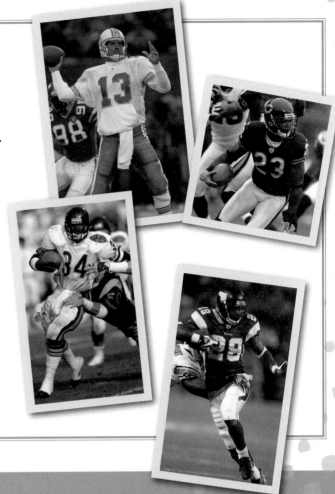

# One Big Play

Records can be set on one play, in one game, or over a season. But one play in the 2007 season combined more records than any other! In the final game of the regular season, the Patriots were trailing the New York Giants. They had to win to finish with a perfect regular-season record. In the fourth quarter, Tom Brady dropped back and heaved a long bomb downfield. A streaking Randy Moss nabbed the ball for a 65-yard touchdown. That one play brought together three amazing records:

☆ **Tom Brady** set a new record with his 50th touchdown pass.

☆ **Randy Moss** set a new record with his 23rd touchdown catch.

☆ **The Patriots** added to their all-time record for points, which ended up at 589!

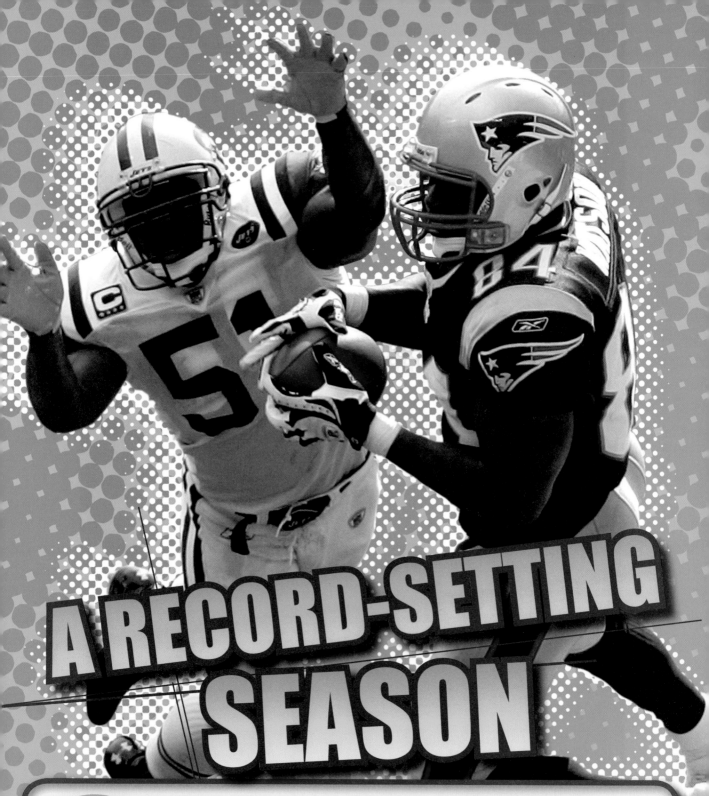

# A RECORD-SETTING SEASON

**S**ee if you can guess what these numbers are: 38, 38, 38, 34, 34, 48, 49, 52. No, they're not a combination for the world's biggest lock. Those are the game-winning point totals for the New England Patriots in the first eight games of the 2007 season. They added a 56-point win in week 10, plus three more games with 30 or more points. By the time the smoke had cleared after their 16 regular-season games, the Pats had scored 589 points, more than any team ever!

## BY THE NUMBERS

Just about everything the Patriots did in 2007 added a new page to the NFL record book. Here are just a few of their amazing stats:

⭐ Most wins in the regular season: 16

⭐ Most wins in a row during the regular season (dating back to 2006): 19

⭐ Tied for most different players to score at least one touchdown: 21

⭐ Most points per game ever: 36.8

⭐ Most points by a road team since 1973 (vs. Buffalo): 56

## TD!

The point of football is to score touchdowns. The Patriots scored more of them in one season than any other team in history! Here are the top all-time TD-happy teams:

| TDs | Team | Year |
| --- | --- | --- |
| 75 | New England Patriots | 2007 |
| 70 | Miami Dolphins | 1984 |
| 67 | St. Louis Rams | 2000 |
| 66 | Four teams have reached this total | |

# Points Patrol

The old record for most points in a season was set by the 1998 Minnesota Vikings. Thanks to their high-powered offense, they scored 556 points. One of the key players for them: Randy Moss!

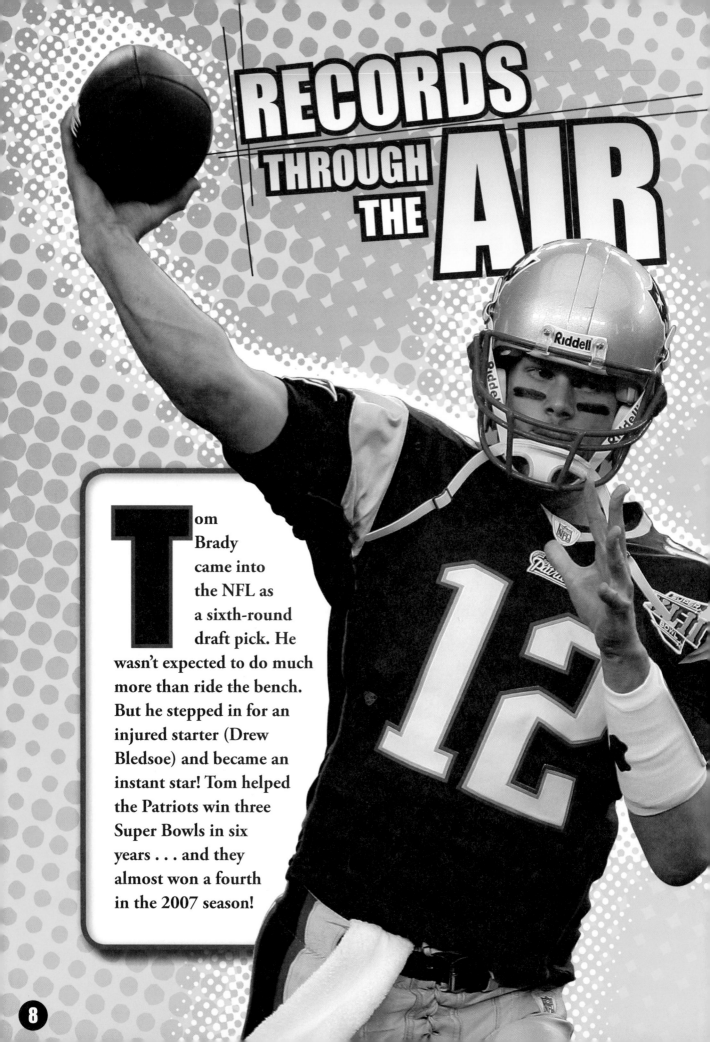

# RECORDS THROUGH THE AIR

**T**om Brady came into the NFL as a sixth-round draft pick. He wasn't expected to do much more than ride the bench. But he stepped in for an injured starter (Drew Bledsoe) and became an instant star! Tom helped the Patriots win three Super Bowls in six years . . . and they almost won a fourth in the 2007 season!

long the way, Tom's found his own place in the NFL record books. The mark for most touchdown passes in season stood at 48 for 20 years. Then Peyton Manning threw for 49 scores in 2004. Most experts thought that number would hold up for quite a while. They didn't count on Tom Terrific!

In 2007, Brady threw at least three touchdown passes in each of his first eight games. He started hot and just kept burning up his opponents. He tied Manning's record in the second quarter of the team's final game. Then, with a 65-yard bomb, Brady passed them all. . . 50 TD passes!

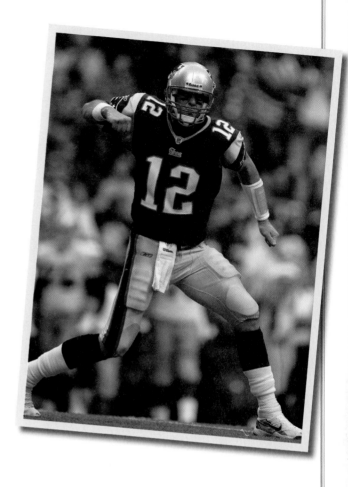

# An Unbroken Record

Brady and Manning have pushed Dan Marino out of the record book. But no one has figured out a way to knock out Johnny Unitas. The great "Johnny U" threw a touchdown pass in 47 straight games! No one else has come within a dozen games of that amazing record. If Tom Brady wants that record, he has to throw touchdown passes in every game for almost the next three seasons! This is one record that might never be broken.

# FANTASTIC FAVRE!

**T**om Brady was not the only superstar QB to have a great 2007 season. Brett Favre of the Green Bay Packers was a veteran star when Brady started his NFL career. In 2007, Favre showed that at the age of 38, he still had the skills!

## TOUCHDOWN PASSES

While Brady and Manning have put up single-season records, Brett now holds the career record. On September 30, 2007, he fired a 16-yard pass to Greg Jennings. When Jennings hit the end zone, Favre hit the record book. It was his 421$^{st}$ career touchdown pass. That snapped the mark of 420 held by Dan Marino. Brett finished the 2007 season with 442 career TD passes.

## PASSING YARDS

The hits kept coming for Brett. Against the Rams, he tossed a seven-yard pass in the second quarter. It was a slant to Donald Driver. With those seven yards, Brett overcame the old career passing record held by Dan Marino. (Ol' Dan had a tough year in the records department!) Favre finished 2007 with an amazing 61,655 career passing yards. How much is that? More than 34 MILES of passes!

## WINS

A quarterback's most important job is to lead his team to victory.

In 2007, Brett passed Broncos great John Elway to become the winningest QB in NFL history. Brett has now been under center for 160 Packers wins.

# Frantastic!

Before Marino and Favre came along to knock him out of the record books, Fran Tarkenton held just about every career passing record. When he retired in 1978, he was the all-time leader in TD passes (342), passing yards (47,003), attempts (6,467), and completions (3,686). The Hall of Famer has lost all those records since, but you know what they say: Records are made to be broken!

# SUPER BOWL PASSING RECORDS

**M**ore than 97 million people in the U.S. watched Eli Manning lead the Giants to victory in Super Bowl XLII. Eli was a master, guiding his team downfield in the final minute to the winning score. But he wasn't the first QB to do that. In Super Bowl XXIII, San Francisco's Joe Montana hit John Taylor with a game-winning TD pass with just 34 seconds left! Let's take a look at other great Super Bowl passing stars:

## TOUCHDOWN PASSES

Joe Montana had 11 TD passes in four games (yes, he won them all!). The most TD passes in one game was 6 by Steve Young of San Francisco in Super Bowl XXIX.

## PASSING YARDS

There's that Joe again.... Montana rolled up 1,142 passing yards in four games. In Super Bowl XXXIV, Kurt Warner of the St. Louis Rams passed for 414 yards, a single-game Super Bowl record.

## COMPLETIONS

While Tom Brady didn't win his most recent Super Bowl, he has won three others. And during Super Bowl XLII, he passed Joe Montana to take over the all-time lead for passes completed in Super Bowls. Tom's at an even 100 (and counting, he hopes!)

## LONGEST PASS PLAY.

Jake Delhomme of the Carolina Panthers didn't lead his team to victory in Super Bowl XXXVIII. But he did find a place in the record book. His 85-yard touchdown strike to Muhsin Muhammad was the longest pass play in Super Bowl history!

# Interceptions:

You didn't think we'd let these QBs get away without talking about INTs, did you? No one likes interceptions (except defensive backs!), but they're part of the game. John Elway of the Denver Broncos lost three Super Bowls before he won two. Along the way, he set the record by tossing eight passes to the wrong teams! Rich Gannon threw five "picks" in Super Bowl XXXVII for a single-game record he wishes he didn't hold!

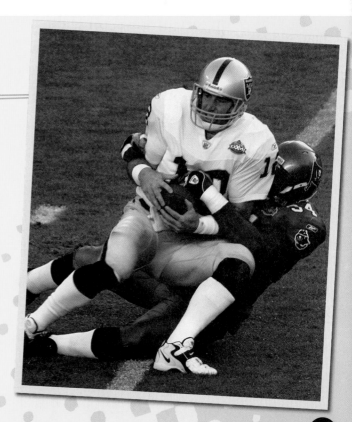

**B**eing a great running back demands strength, speed, stamina . . . and bravery. You get help from your blockers, but once the rock's in your hands, it's all up to you. Running backs find their way into the record books in two important ways: touchdowns and rushing yards. In recent years, the touchdown record has been changed so often, we hope that it was written in pencil! Who will erase it next?

# RUSHING TO THE RECORD

# Big Gainers

The stat called "yards from scrimmage" adds up a player's totals for rushing and receiving yards. In recent seasons, several players have made racked up some of the highest single-season marks of all time! * means still playing!

| Player | Yards from Scrimmage | Year |
| --- | --- | --- |
| Marshall Faulk, Rams | 2,429 | 1999 |
| Tiki Barber, Giants | 2,390 | 2005 |
| LaDainian Tomlinson*, Chargers | 2,370 | 2003 |
| Barry Sanders, Lions | 2,358 | 1997 |
| Steven Jackson*, Rams | 2,334 | 2006 |
| LaDainian Tomlinson*, Chargers | 2,323 | 2006 |

### LT = TD!

During 2006, no one could stop LT! LaDainian Tomlinson was a scoring machine for San Diego. He scored 31 touchdowns to set a new single-season record. LT's total of 186 points broke a record set in 1961! Not all were rushing TDs, but any score is a good score! LT streaked to 100 career rushing TDs faster than anyone else, too! He's third on the all-time list with 115 TDs on the ground. He's got a long way to go to catch all-time leader Emmitt Smith, who has 164!

### BEFORE LT

LT's 31 touchdowns were the most ever. But he was breaking a record that has been broken a lot in recent years. Emmitt Smith scored 25 times in 1995. But that number was topped four times, starting in 2000. Marshall Faulk of the Rams made it 26 that year. In 2003, Priest Holmes of the Chiefs raised it to 27. On his way to a spot in the Super Bowl, Shaun Alexander of the Seahawks made it 28. Finally, LT topped them all in 2006 with his 31 scores. At this rate, the record will be 50 by the time you have a chance to break it yourself!

### RUMBLING ALONG

LT has gained at least 1,200 yards in each of his first seven seasons. In the long history of the NFL, only the great Eric Dickerson has previously done that.

BOOK

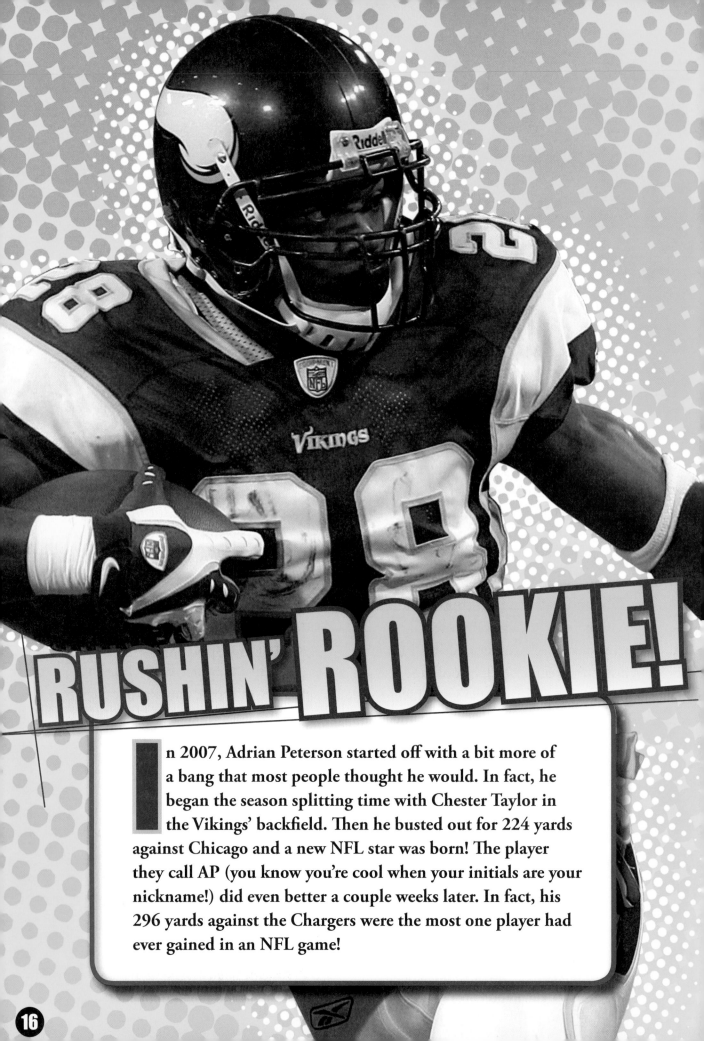

# RUSHIN' ROOKIE!

In 2007, Adrian Peterson started off with a bit more of a bang that most people thought he would. In fact, he began the season splitting time with Chester Taylor in the Vikings' backfield. Then he busted out for 224 yards against Chicago and a new NFL star was born! The player they call AP (you know you're cool when your initials are your nickname!) did even better a couple weeks later. In fact, his 296 yards against the Chargers were the most one player had ever gained in an NFL game!

## BIG GAMES

**Here are the biggest single-game rushing totals in NFL history:**

| Player | Yards | Year |
| --- | --- | --- |
| Adrian Peterson | 296 | 2007 |
| Jamal Lewis | 295 | 2003 |
| Corey Dillon | 278 | 2000 |
| Walter Payton | 275 | 1977 |

# Quite a Game!

In the same game that **AP** set the rushing record, San Diego's Antonio Cromartie set a record that can never be broken! He returned an interception 109 yards for a touchdown. That's the longest-possible return, so Antonio's mark can only be tied . . . not topped!

## LONG TIME RUNNING

As great as AP and LT are, they're still a long way from the top of the NFL's career rushing list. In fact, among all active NFL runners, only Edgerrin James of the Cardinals is within 7,000 yards of Emmitt Smith's all-time record! Here's a list of the runners who have rumbled for the most yards ever. All are in the Pro Football Hall of Fame (or will be when their time to be voted in comes along . . . ).

| Player | Yards |
| --- | --- |
| Emmitt Smith | 18,355 |
| Walter Payton | 16,726 |
| Barry Sanders | 15,269 |
| Curtis Martin | 14,101 |
| Jerome Bettis | 13,662 |
| Eric Dickerson | 13,259 |
| Tony Dorsett | 12,739 |
| Jim Brown | 12,312 |
| Marshall Faulk | 12,279 |
| Marcus Allen | 12,243 |

# SUPER BOWL RUSHING
# RECORDS

Super Bowl is the biggest pressure cooker in sports. Though passers have often been the biggest stars, running backs have certainly made their marks.

## FRANCO FOREVER!

In the 1970s, the Pittsburgh Steelers won four Super Bowls. Leading the way was a powerful runner whose success in the big games carved his name in the record books. Franco Harris ran for more yards in Super Bowls (354), while carrying the ball more times (101) than anyone else. He scored five times in those games. Only Emmitt Smith of Dallas has been able to tie that rushing TD record.

## SINGLE-GAME STARS

Which runners have shined brightest on the Super Bowl stage? The most yards ever gained by one player in a Super Bowl was 204 by Washington's Timmy Smith. The young runner never gained that many yards in a game before or after. But for the Redskins Super Bowl XXII win over Denver, Smith was really super!

Terrell Davis ran for a single-game record of three touchdowns in 1998 when Denver won its first Super Bowl. The man with the right initials—TD—scored on three one-yard runs as the Broncos won Super Bowl XXXII 31-24.

## LONGEST RUN

There have been dozens of great runs in Super Bowl history, but only one of them was the longest ever. The speedy owner of that record is Pittsburgh's Willie Parker. He sped 75 yards for a touchdown in Super Bowl XL as the Steelers beat the Seahawks.

# Bad Day on the Ground

These pages celebrate great runners in the Super Bowl. But let's look at the other side of the ball, too. In Super Bowl **XX**, the Chicago Bears held the New England Patriots to only 7 yards rushing! That's not even enough for one first down! No surprise here: the Bears dominated 46-10.

# CATCHING THE RECORDS

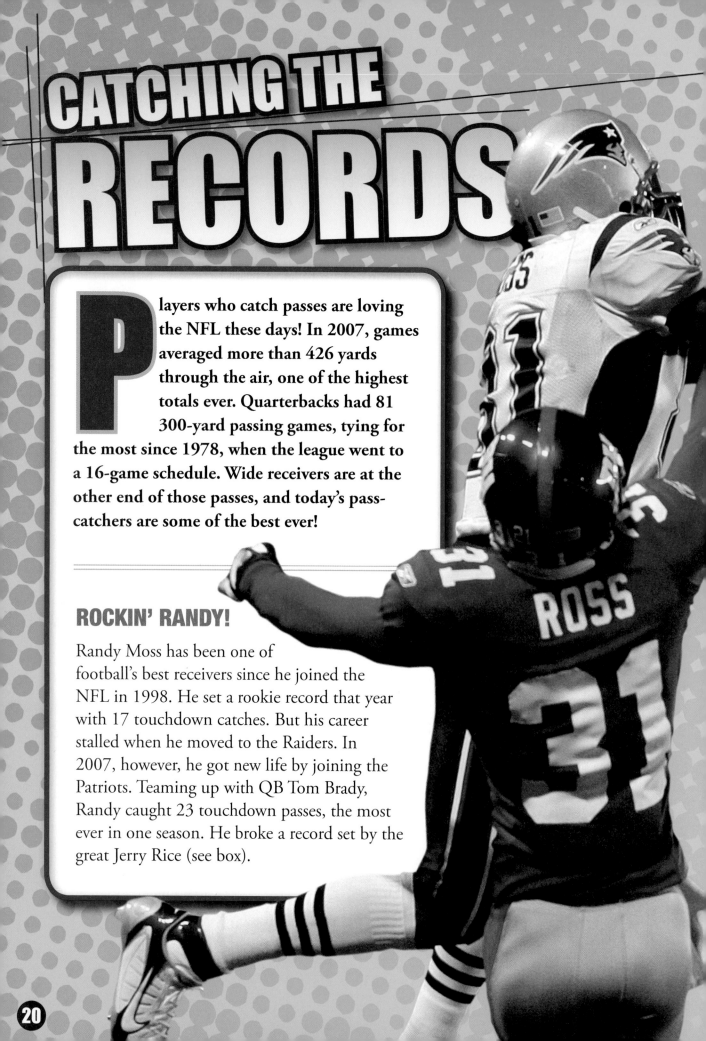

**P**layers who catch passes are loving the NFL these days! In 2007, games averaged more than 426 yards through the air, one of the highest totals ever. Quarterbacks had 81 300-yard passing games, tying for the most since 1978, when the league went to a 16-game schedule. Wide receivers are at the other end of those passes, and today's pass-catchers are some of the best ever!

## ROCKIN' RANDY!

Randy Moss has been one of football's best receivers since he joined the NFL in 1998. He set a rookie record that year with 17 touchdown catches. But his career stalled when he moved to the Raiders. In 2007, however, he got new life by joining the Patriots. Teaming up with QB Tom Brady, Randy caught 23 touchdown passes, the most ever in one season. He broke a record set by the great Jerry Rice (see box).

## YOUNG STARS

A trio of young receivers have their eyes on the records set by Moss and Rice. Keep an eye on these guys in the future . . . NFL defensive backs certainly will, too!

⭐ Anquan Boldin: Reached 400 career catches in only 67 games, fastest ever!

⭐ Marques Colston: His 168 catches were the most ever by a receiver in his first two seasons.

⭐ T.J. Houshmandzadeh: Caught a touchdown in the first eight games of 2007, the second-longest streak ever.

## TERRIFIC TEAM-UP

Of course, it takes two players to make a touchdown pass. Heading into 2007, the duos of Dan Marino and Mark Clayton of the 1984 Dolphins, and Brett Favre and Sterling Sharpe of the 1994 Packers each teamed up for 18 scores.

# Jerry Rice: By the Numbers

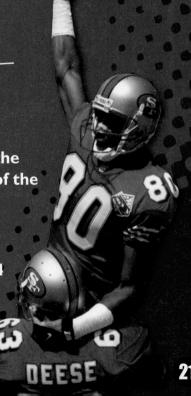

Today's pass-catchers are certainly having their day. But they're all still chasing the player who holds more receiving records than anyone. Jerry Rice starred for the San Francisco 49ers from 1985-2004. Here are some of the amazing pass-catching marks he racked up:

⭐ **Most career receiving touchdowns:** 197
⭐ **Most games in a row with at least one catch:** 274
⭐ **Most catches:** 1,1549
⭐ **Most receiving yards in a year:** 1,848
⭐ **Most career receiving yards:** 22,895

# GOOD THING HE SWITCHED!

**T**ony Gonzalez was a top basketball player in college at the University of California at Berkeley. But he was also a great football player. Which way should he go? Tony decided to stick with football, and Kansas City Chiefs fans are still thanking him for that choice. He has become one of the greatest tight ends in NFL history.

In 2007, Tony had another awesome season, while adding to his career totals. With 66 career touchdown catches, he set a new all-time record for TEs. He broke the old record of 62 held by Denver great Shannon Sharpe.

Tony also passed Shannon in another category. Tony's 820 career catches are now the most ever by a TE, topping Shannon's 815 grabs.

## 2007:
## YEAR OF THE TIGHT END

For only the second time ever, three tight ends had more than 1,000 yards receiving. And had Antonio Gates gotten just 16 more yards, he would have been in that group as well.

| Player | Team | Yards |
| --- | --- | --- |
| Jason Witten, | Dallas, | 1,145 |
| Tony Gonzalez, | Kansas City, | 1,172 |
| Kellen Winslow, | Cleveland, | 1,106 |

## MORE SD TDS

While running back LaDainian "LT" Tomlinson gets most of the headlines in San Diego, tight end Antonio Gates is also breaking records. In 2004, he set an all-time record among TEs by grabbing 13 touchdown catches.

## All-Time Ozzie

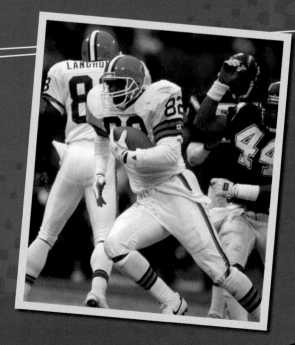

Before Shannon Sharpe and Tony Gonzalez came along to break his records, Ozzie Newsome was the NFL's top tight end. Ozzie played for Cleveland from 1978 through 1990. Big, tall, and fast, he changed the way tight ends were used. His career totals of 662 catches and 7,980 yards were the most ever when he retired. He was elected to the Hall of Fame in 1999. Today, he is the general manager of the Baltimore Ravens.

# SUPER BOWL RECEIVING RECORDS

On old-time merry-go-rounds, if you grabbed a brass ring as you spun around, you'd win a free ride. For NFL players, the "brass ring" has the words "Super Bowl" on it. They work constantly to be able to grab one. Some players grab a lot of footballs on their way to Super Bowl glory. Here's a look at the pass-catching stars of football's biggest game.

## MOST RECEIVING YARDS

Not surprisingly, the greatest receiver in NFL history is also the most successful receiver in Super Bowl history. Jerry Rice helped the 49ers win four Super Bowls in the 1980s. His smooth style helped him carve defenses to shreds. Jerry caught passes for a Super Bowl career record 589 yards. In Super Bowl XXIII, he set the single-game record with 215 receiving yards.

## MOST CATCHES

One guess who holds the records in this category: Jerry Rice! Jerry hauled in 33 receptions in his four Super Bowls. In Super Bowl XXIII, he tied a record set by Cincinnati's Dan Ross in Super Bowl XVI with 11 catches. In the past four Super Bowls, a pair of sure-handed targets have tied that record. New England's Deion Branch had 11 catches on his way to Super Bowl XXXIX MVP trophy. Another Patriots, Wes Welker also had 11 catches in a losing effort in Super Bowl XLII.

## MOST RECEIVING TDS

It's a clean sweep of key receiving records for the amazing Rice. He had eight touchdown catches in Super Bowl play. In fact, no one else has even three! And Jerry set the single-game record with three scoring grabs in Super Bowl XXIX!

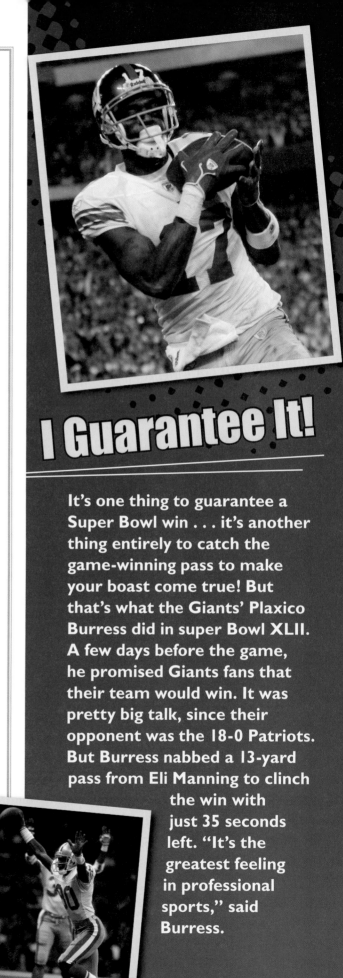

# I Guarantee It!

It's one thing to guarantee a Super Bowl win . . . it's another thing entirely to catch the game-winning pass to make your boast come true! But that's what the Giants' Plaxico Burress did in super Bowl XLII. A few days before the game, he promised Giants fans that their team would win. It was pretty big talk, since their opponent was the 18-0 Patriots. But Burress nabbed a 13-yard pass from Eli Manning to clinch the win with just 35 seconds left. "It's the greatest feeling in professional sports," said Burress.

# KICKS AND RETURNS

### HESTER RUNS AWAY WITH SEASON

Devin Hester of the Chicago Bears had a great rookie season in 2006, when he set a record by returning five kicks for touchdowns. He added one more during the Bears' Super Bowl XLI loss. But guess what? He was just getting started. He topped his rookie year by returning six more kicks for scores in 2007. His four punt returns among that total tied for the most ever in one season. Few players in NFL history have brought as much excitement to special teams as Hester.

### HOBBS KICKS OFF SEASON

Normally, when a player receives a kickoff deep in the end zone, he takes a knee for a touchback. He doesn't run it back out, and his team starts on their own 20. It's the safe play. But Ellis Hobbs didn't want the Patriots' season to start safe in 2007. Snagging the opening-game second-half kickoff eight yards deep in his own end zone, he returned it 108 yards for a touchdown. For a few weeks, it was the longest play in NFL history! It's still tied for the longest kickoff return, but an interception return later in 2007 snapped Hobbs' mark for longest play (see page 17).

## GALE FORCE

Many fans compare Devin Hester to another amazing Chicago Bears player. Gale Sayers combined speed and great moves like few players before or since. Though his career was cut short by knee injuries, he made the Hall of Fame anyway. During the five years he returned kicks, he brought back eight for TDs. His greatest day came in his rookie season, 1965. He had an 85-yard punt return for a score on a day when he hit the end zone six times! That tied an all-time record for one game.

## IT'S GOOD, GOOD, GOOD, GOOD, GOOD, GOOD, GOOD, AND GOOD!

Against the Houston Texans on October 21, 2007, Tennessee was pretty happy that it had Rob Bironas on its side. The right-footed kicker booted an NFL-

record of eight field goals! That total broke the old mark, set by four other kickers, by one. To cap off his amazing day, Rob added two extra points, giving him 26 points, the most ever scored by a kicker in one game!

## LONG DISTANCE!

Making one field goal of more than 50 yards in a game can make a kicker a hero. Making two can earn him a raise. So what did Kris Brown get for making three 50-plus three-pointers? A ride off the field! After earlier hitting a pair of 54-yard kicks, Kris angled in a 57-yard field goal on the final play to give the Texans a victory!

# A Raider Boomer

Punters don't get much attention when it comes to records. But when one becomes the all-time best, it's worth a mention. In 2007, Shane Lechler of the Raiders had a 41.1-yard net punting average. That topped the old mark of 39.9 by the Giants' Mike Horan in 1993. Net punting is how far Shane punted minus how far the ball was returned. Shane pinned Oakland's opponents back there better than anyone else ever has!

# RECORDS FOR THE DEFENSE

## SACK MASTERS!

**S**acks have been part of the NFL since the first time a quarterback dropped back to pass. However, the league has only been officially counting them since 1982. Since then, the NFL's top linemen have made their money chasing down QBs.

Michael Strahan added a Super Bowl championship to his great career, when his Giants beat the Patriots in Super Bowl XLII. The Giants' sacks of Tom Brady played a big part in that win. Strahan knows all about big sacks. In 2001, he set the all-time single-season record with 22.5 sacks. (How do you get half a sack? If you and a teammate both tackle the QB at the same time, you each get a half.)

Strahan has more sacks than any other active player. But he has a long way to go to catch the all-time leader. Mighty Bruce Smith piled up 200 sacks from 1985-2003 on his way to the Hall of Fame. Smith also had an NFL-best: 13 seasons with 10 or more sacks.

# Fumble = Touchdown!

Defensive players love almost nothing more than whacking a ballcarrier and causing a fumble. We said "almost" nothing—one thing they like better is finding a football lying around on the field and then taking it to the end zone. A fumble returned for a score can be a huge, game-changing play. In NFL history, no one has returned more fumbles for scores than Miami's awesome defensive end Jason Taylor with five. Taylor, a former NFL defensive player of the year, combines speed and a nose for the ball like few players ever. If the ball's on the ground . . . look for Jason to come swooping in!

## DOUBLE THREAT

Defensive backs are expected to make interceptions. It's a big part of their job. But only one player has picked off at least 30 passes while also making 30 sacks in his career! Rodney Harrison of the New England Patriots became the first player to reach both of those totals amid the Pats' amazing 2007 season. It takes a special talent to be able to back up and make a pick, and also charge forward to sack the QB.

# SUPER BOWL DEFENSE AND SPECIAL TEAMS

**A** big special-teams play in the big game can mean the difference between a Super Bowl ring and an empty finger. Plus, every coach will tell you, "defense wins championships." Let's look at some record-setting Super Bowl performers on special teams and "D."

# Giant-Sized D!

We'll wrap up our look at **NFL** records with a peek at why **New England** didn't set the record for having an undefeated season. The answer can be summed up in two words: **Dee Fense!** The Giants defense simply knocked the Patriots around, especially QB **Tom Brady.** They had five sacks (two short of the single-game record) and forced Brady to fumble once. They also had a dozen "hurries." That is, they pressured him so much he threw early or poorly. Plus they held the Pats to only 45 yards rushing. All that was left was to throw a Giant-sized party in New York City!

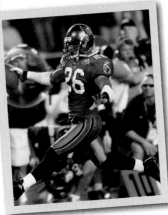

## RETURNING MVP

Only one kick-returner has been named the Most Valuable Player of a Super Bowl. In Super Bowl XXXI, the Packers' Desmond Howard was one of the smallest players on the field. But he made some of the biggest plays! First, he set up the Packers' first score with a 32-yard punt return. Another 24-yard return led to a Packers' field goal. Then, after the Patriots scored to pull within six points, Howard set a Super Bowl record with a 99-yard kickoff return for the clinching score.

## TAMPA BAY'S BIG DAY

The Tampa Bay Buccaneers defense was considered the NFL's best in 2002. They carried the team into Super Bowl XXXVII against the Oakland Raiders. There they put on a show, holding a powerful Oakland offense to just 19 yards and one first down on the ground. They also dominated in the air, too, intercepting Raiders' QB Rich Gannon a record-setting five times! In the third quarter, Tampa's Dwight Smith returned a pick for a commanding 34-3 lead. During the fourth quarter, Derrick Brooks and then Smith again returned interceptions for scores. The trio of end-zone trips also set a Super Bowl record!

# Oops!
## Records Nobody Wants

Getting his name in the NFL record book can make any player happy . . . almost any player, that is. While most records celebrate great accomplishments by players or teams, other records mark less-than-successful moments. Here are a few players who hold spots in the NFL record book that they probably wish they didn't!

### BUTTERFINGERS!

Quarterbacks handle the ball over and over in a game. So it's no surprise they also mishandle it most often. Here are four butterfingered champs:

Warren Moon is in the Pro Football Hall of Fame thanks to his awesome passing. He's in the Hall of Shame for setting an all-time record with 161 career fumbles!

Kerry Collins and Daunte Culpepper both led their teams to the playoffs several times. But they also dropped the ball—literally!—more times in a season than anyone else. Collins booted the pigskin 23 times in 2001. Culpepper "lost the handle" the same amount the following season.

Len Dawson is also in the Hall of Fame. But one game he probably wishes he had stayed home for came in 1964. Playing for the Kansas City Chiefs, Dawson fumbled seven times that day . . . another all-time "oops" record.

### HARDY DO THAT?

During a game against the Eagles in 1950, Cardinals quarterback Jim Hardy must have gotten his team's uniform mixed up with his opponents'. Hardy threw a record eight passes to the Eagles . . . an all-time high (or low!) for interceptions in a game.

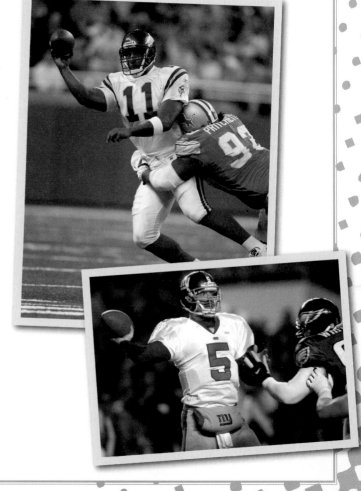